I0825462

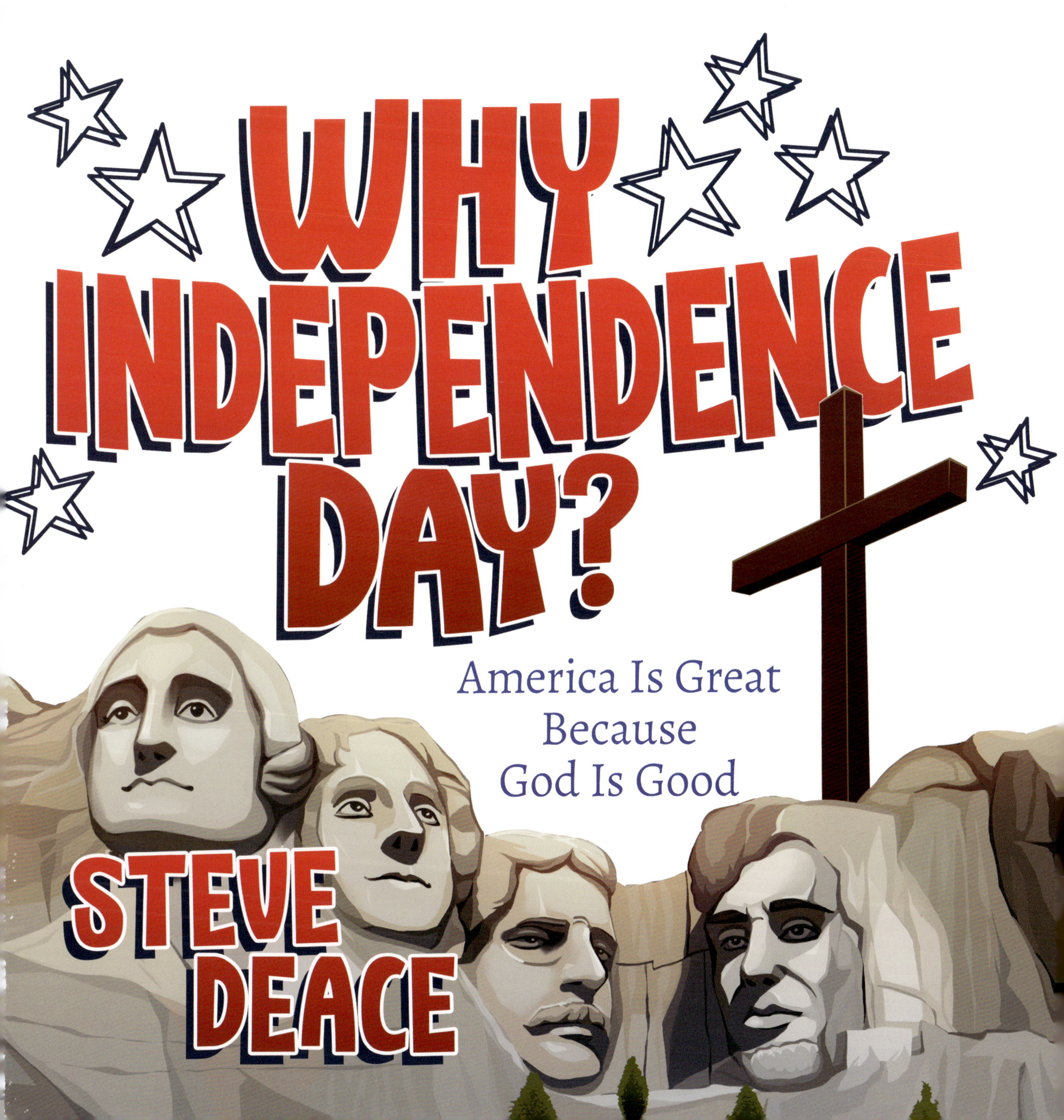
WHY INDEPENDENCE DAY?
America Is Great
Because
God Is Good
STEVE DEACE

A POST HILL PRESS BOOK
ISBN: 979-8-89565-594-8

Why Independence Day?:
America Is Great Because God Is Good

Interior Design by Alana Mills

Post Hill Press
New York • Nashville
posthillpress.com

Published in the United States of America
1 2 3 4 5 6 7 8 9 10
Printed in Canada

For Amy, the best mother for my children

America is a special place to live. We are lucky to live in a free country where many people around the world wish they could live. But why is America so special?

To understand what makes America so special, we have to go way back in time, long ago to the beginning of another special land.

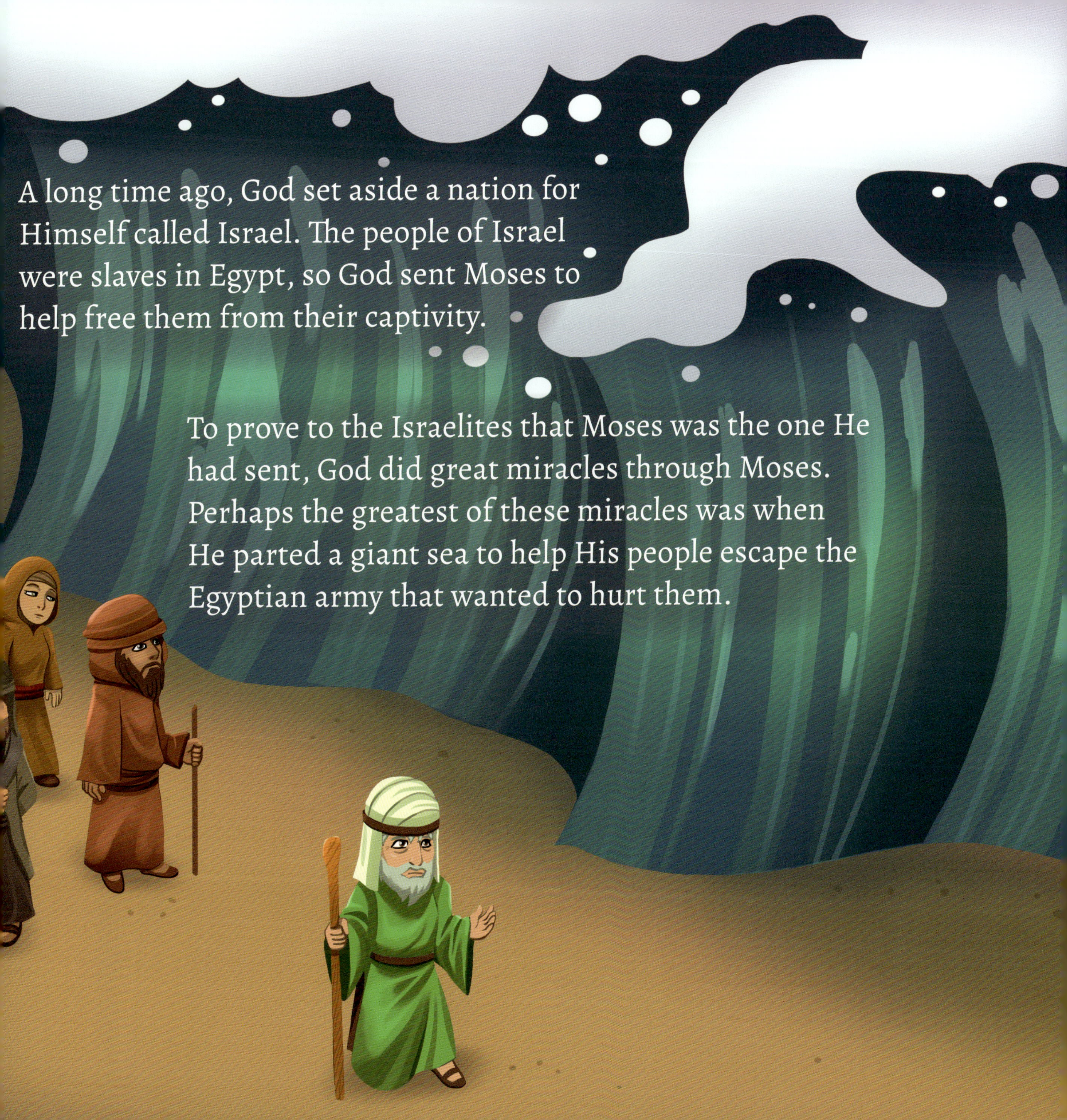

A long time ago, God set aside a nation for Himself called Israel. The people of Israel were slaves in Egypt, so God sent Moses to help free them from their captivity.

To prove to the Israelites that Moses was the one He had sent, God did great miracles through Moses. Perhaps the greatest of these miracles was when He parted a giant sea to help His people escape the Egyptian army that wanted to hurt them.

After a few months of traveling to safety, God called Moses to the top of a very high mountain to give him another miracle, the Ten Commandments.

These were the first words God had ever written by His own hand. And to show they were to be forever, God wrote them into a stone that could never be erased.

These Ten Commandments told God's people for the first time what was right and what was wrong. And God wanted the Israelites to share these Commandments with the rest of the world too!

Since God made us and loves us, He wanted everyone to know His ways so we wouldn't do bad things that harm ourselves or others.

I
II
III
IV
V
VI
VII
VIII
IX
X

That is why when you visit Washington, DC, our nation's capital, you still see statues and paintings of Moses today, many, many years later.

Moses on the Supreme Court Building

Moses at the Library of Congress

They are there to remind us that our laws are based on God's laws, for He knows what is right and what is wrong better than anyone else. Since no one could possibly love us more than God does, we know He always wants what's best for us. And we are always better off listening to Him.

But that's not the only important thing that happened in Israel that inspired America. Many years after Moses went up to the mountain to hear from God, God came down to earth to meet us in the form of a baby named Jesus Christ.

While He grew up, Jesus lived a perfect life, free of sin. He taught the Gospel and showed us how we should live our lives to honor God. He said that since we couldn't get to Heaven, Heaven came to us.

This is why we celebrate Christmas and why we give each other Christmas gifts, in honor of God giving us the greatest gift—His one and only Son.

Just as Moses freed the people of Israel from slavery in Egypt, Jesus came and freed all of us from wanting to do bad things and disobey God. Jesus suffered and died for us on the Cross, taking all of the punishment we deserved for the bad stuff we did and still do to ourselves and each other.

And then He rose again on the third day, the day we call Easter, to show that we can now live forever with God, as long as we trust and believe in Jesus.

After Jesus went back to Heaven, He sent a special helper called the Holy Spirit to live inside us. This helper allows us to understand God better and do good things.

You can tell you have the Holy Spirit in you if you want to say no to bad things, or if you want to ask God for forgiveness when you make a mistake.

The Holy Spirit also makes us want to pray for others! It's like having a special friend inside you who always wants to help you be good.

Now that His people had the Holy Spirit, it became easier to spread the message of Jesus all over the world. It was like a special gift that helped people understand and believe in Jesus, even without things like TV or computers.

Over the next one thousand years, Christianity became the biggest religion in history, and it still is today!

This shows that what they were saying was really true, because only God's truth and power could make something spread so far without any fancy tools.

But not everyone was happy that the message of Jesus was spreading all over the world.

There were some powerful people who didn't know about God's love, or didn't like His love because they wanted everyone to think *they* were more important, like gods themselves.

Because of this, some of the people who loved Jesus and wanted to follow Him were treated very, very unkindly. They were sometimes hurt or even put in jail, for no good reason at all.

One special group of these brave Christians, who wanted more than anything to obey God, was called the Puritans.

It was around this time that a brave and famous explorer named Christopher Columbus discovered what was called the "New World."

It was an entirely new continent that Christians had never visited before. Lots of brave explorers sailed the big ocean, just like Christopher Columbus!

And guess what? This new land was given a special name that it still has today: America!

Now, the Puritans were a group who loved God very much. But their king was very mean and wouldn't let them live the way God wanted them to.

So, with brave hearts and prayers, they decided to sail all the way across the big ocean to this new place called America! They hoped they could live happily ever after there, following God's rules without anyone being mean to them.

The brave Puritans boarded a ship called the *Mayflower*. The journey was long and very scary, but they were excited to begin a new life and had faith God would help.

They finally landed and made their settlement in a place they called the Plymouth Colony, which later became part of the state of Massachusetts!

After arriving, they wrote rules for how everyone should live together. They called it the *Mayflower Compact*. This was important because it marked the beginning of the country we live in today.

The Mayflower Compact

FRENCH TERRITORY
MASSACHUSETTS
N.H.
NEW YORK
CONN.
RHODE ISLAND
PENNSYLVANIA
NEWJERSEY
FRENCH TERRITORY
DELAWARE
MARYLAND
VIRGINIA
NORTH CAROLINA
SOUTH CAROLINA
GEORGIA
SPANISH TERRITORY
ALTANTIC OCEAN

As more and more Christians followed the Puritans' example and came to America, they started communities that were called colonies.

Eventually there were thirteen colonies and each and every one of them represented Christianity in their own unique way.

But just like what happened in England, the more Christianity spread in the American colonies, the more the king who owned the colonies became angry.

This is because the more we study God's Word, the Bible, the more we want to be free as God made us to be and not have to follow rules different than God's.

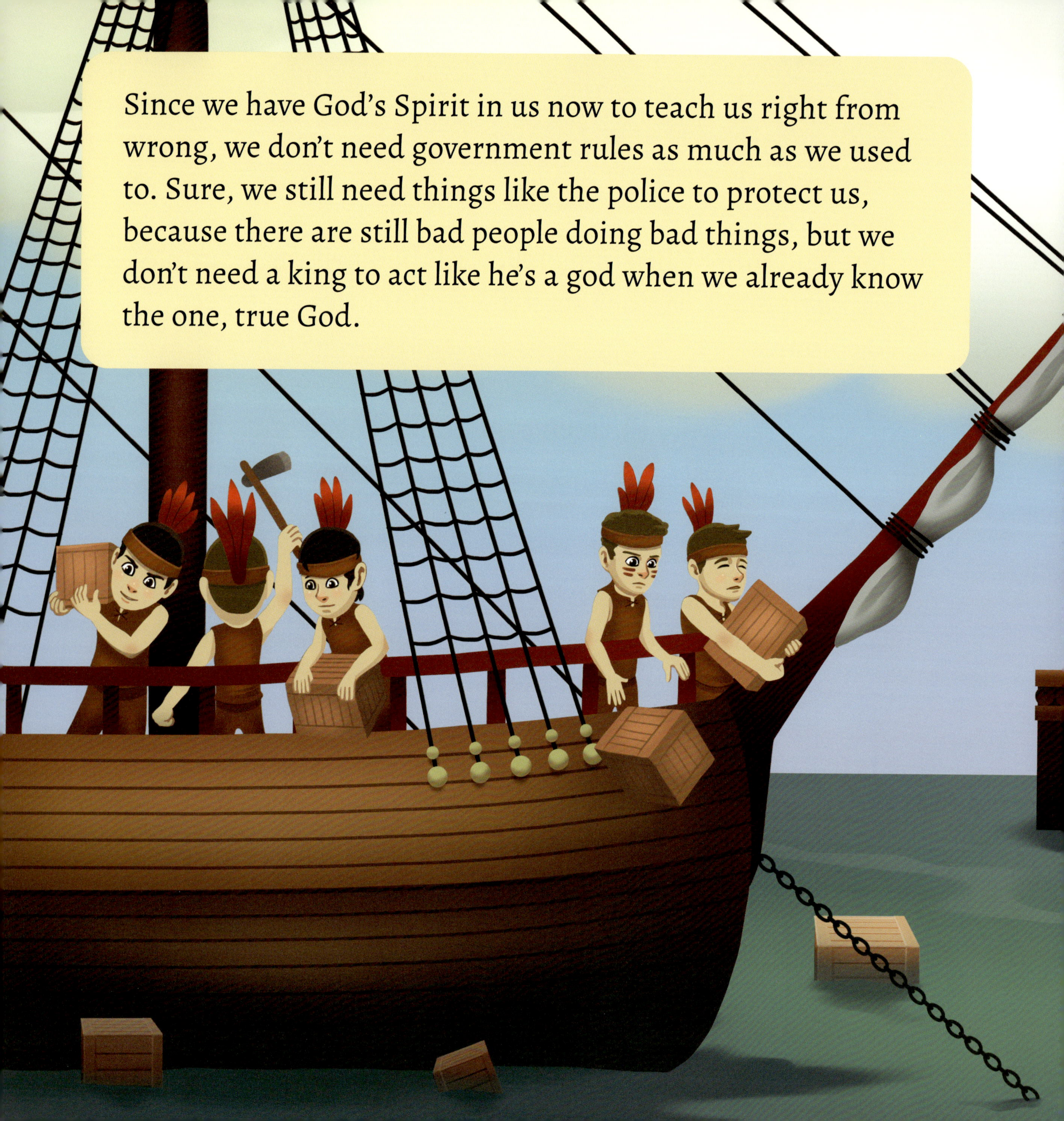

Since we have God's Spirit in us now to teach us right from wrong, we don't need government rules as much as we used to. Sure, we still need things like the police to protect us, because there are still bad people doing bad things, but we don't need a king to act like he's a god when we already know the one, true God.

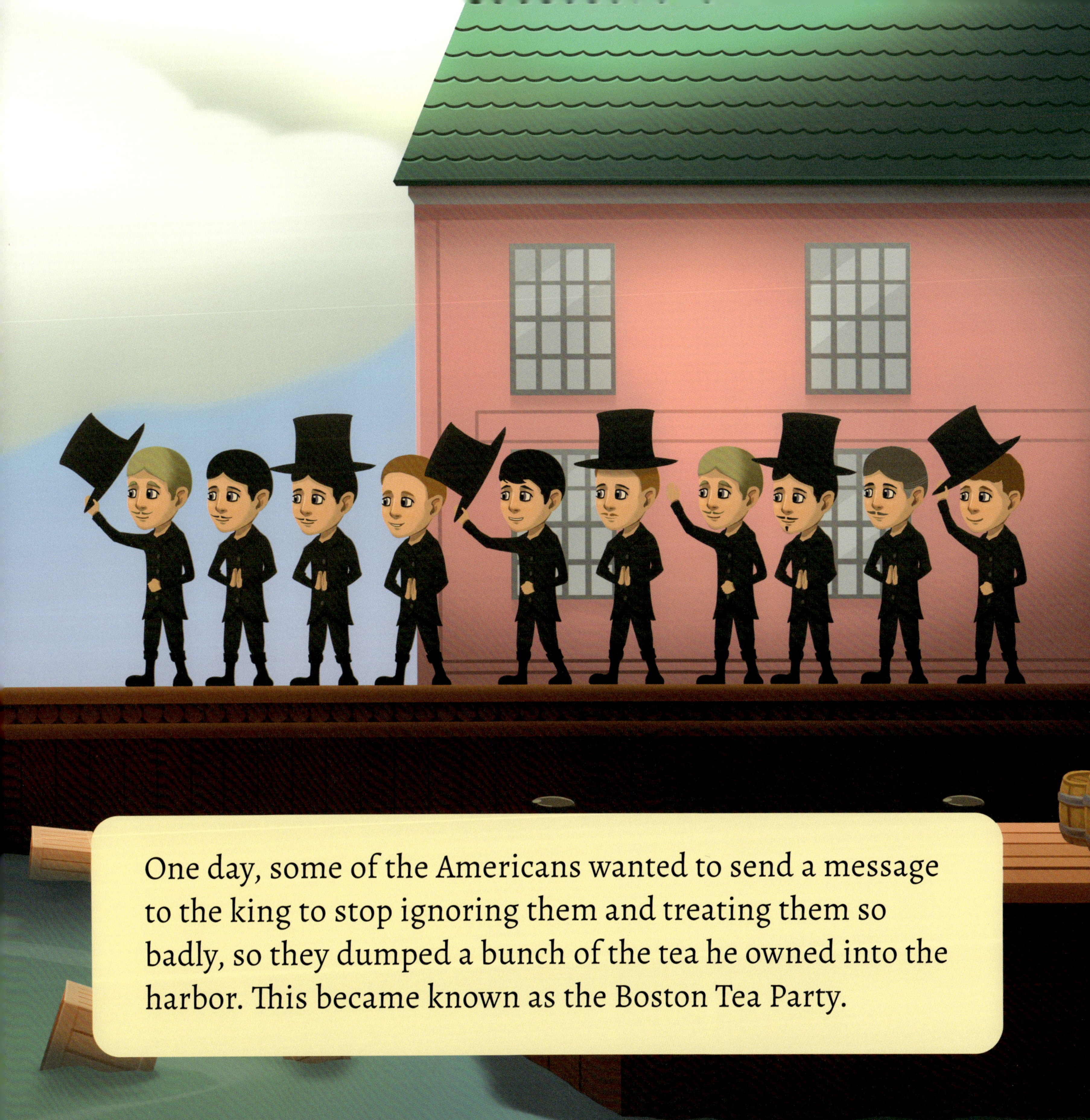

One day, some of the Americans wanted to send a message to the king to stop ignoring them and treating them so badly, so they dumped a bunch of the tea he owned into the harbor. This became known as the Boston Tea Party.

Instead of listening to their concerns, the king became even meaner than he was before! He made it so that the things people needed cost *way* more than they could afford. He even made people keep his soldiers with guns in their homes!

After a long time of the king treating them badly, a group of people came together from all thirteen colonies to talk about what to do about the mean king. These patriots became known as our Founding Fathers.

Finally, they all met up in a city called Philadelphia, and on July 4, 1776, they agreed to what became known as the *Declaration of Independence*.

The *Declaration* was important because it reminded us that as God's people, we have to obey God first. Even if a king tells you to do something that God says is wrong, you should obey God instead of the king.

Since the mean king was forcing the colonists to do things that disobeyed God, they were forced to defy the king by writing the *Declaration* and forming their own country based on what God says.

These thirteen colonies were called the United States of America. This was the day the country you are blessed to be born into and live in began. And it's why we've been celebrating Independence Day on the Fourth of July ever since!

But just like the Pharaoh with Moses, the mean king did not want to let God's people go. So, he brought his army to America to try and take it back over.

They were called the Redcoats for their bright red and scary uniforms, and they were the most powerful army in the world at the time.

Nobody thought our Founding Fathers had a chance. But they had a secret weapon: what they called "providence," or the will of Almighty God. Throughout the war for our Independence, things just seemed to happen that were so lucky it *had* to mean God was doing it.

Like when the great general, George Washington, miraculously crossed an icy river on Christmas night without being seen or heard and was able to surprise the enemy soldiers.

It took almost five years to win the war for our Independence, and there were times it seemed as if hope was lost and the mean king and his Redcoats would win instead.

But it was a blessing in disguise that our Founding Fathers had less soldiers and fewer guns, cannons, and ships than the enemy.

Because it forced them to use other weapons, like the power of praying to Almighty God for Him to help create a country that would bless His Name throughout the world.

God answered their prayers, and sometimes in funny ways. For example, this is one of the few times in history that the French were actually brave and courageous enough to come to our aid. There's no way that would have happened without the will and power of God. We usually have to save the French!

Finally, in January of 1781, the final battle was won in Yorktown, Virginia. The Redcoats gave up and went back home to England. The United States of America was free!

Our Founding Fathers, the Christian men who won the war for our Independence, immediately got back together to pray to God for wisdom and to write the rules for how our country should live in ways that honored God, just as the Puritans had once done.

They came up with what they called the *Constitution*. And it remains the law of our land to this very day!

We the People

Our Founding Fathers wanted our country to be a shining city on a hill, bright and tall for the rest of the world to see. They wanted to inspire people in other parts of the world to follow their example and be free.

This is why other than Christ's Church, where you go to Sunday school, nothing else has done more to spread Christianity and God's Word throughout the world than America has over the last 250 years.

They also wanted future generations of Americans to always remember the true meaning of Independence Day and celebrate it.

Founding Father John Adams suggested Independence Day should be celebrated not only with prayer and devotion to Almighty God, but also with what he called "illuminations."

You call them fireworks, and that's why we still set off awesome fireworks in the sky every July 4th!

As you can see, our Independence Day isn't just the most important day in American history, it is one of the most important days in all of world history.

Because of what the Founding Fathers believed and fought for, America never would have happened without Almighty God, which means America won't be able to continue without Almighty God either.

Previous generations understood it was their duty
to honor God and keep America free.
Now it's our turn.